Psalm 78:4
"We will not hide these truths
from our children but will tell
the next generation about the
glorious deeds of the LORD. We
will tell of his power and the
mighty miracles he did."

The Powers and Mighty Miracles of God

by Karen Erwin Griffith

Printed in the United State of America.

First edition.

The Powers and Mighty Miracles of God.

Summary: Author's stories about God's action in her life.

Title ID: 8913655
ISBN-13: 978-1724588012

Table of Contents

Introduction

For months and months I have been wanting to write a book, but felt stuck. I asked God to show me what to write about over and over again. I asked my small group and others to hold me accountable. I complained to my dear Ed, many times, about how I was stuck and couldn't shake free to write. He bought me a new computer. Still stuck. He bought me a typing table and chair so I would be comfortable. Still stuck.

For the last three years, at the beginning of each, I have asked God to give me a word to guide my life. The first year he gave me "CONTENT". The second year the word was "CONNECT". So I was quite surprised in 2018 to receive the word "HUMILITY". I think that was the beginning of my understanding why I felt stuck – I was stuck in pride. Every idea I had about writing was about me, my accomplishments, my life, my worthiness.

I had stored away several 4" binders full of sermons that I preached during my four years as a pastor in Texas. I was saving them as my legacy for my children. I began going through them, thinking that I could put a book together based on those volumes, but all I discovered was that the ears to hear those words were no longer my audience, and most of them were meaningless outside of the church and the Holy Spirit's interpretation. I realized that keeping them was prideful because they pointed to me and my work rather than God's Word. I threw them all away.

In the summer I was invited to lunch with a friend. I mentioned to her my dilemma and stuck-ness. She, in her wisdom, reminded me that "to everything there is a season" and perhaps, as much as I wanted to write now, it wasn't the season. Her words helped me to let go and be free to really hear from God.

Most of 2018 I had begun my days thanking God, journaling my thanks, praying, and reading from the yearly Bible plan that I have used for years. On July 20 the assigned scriptures were from 1 Thessalonians, 2 Chronicles and Psalm 78. As I began reading from that Psalm, I felt the Holy Spirit setting me free from being stuck.

Psalm 78:1-4 (New Living Testament)

O my people, listen to my teaching

open your ears to what I am saying...

I will teach you hidden lessons from our past –

stories we have heard and know,

stories our ancestors have handed down to us.

We will not hide these truths from our children

but will tell the next generation about the glorious deeds of

the LORD.

We will tell of his powers and the mighty miracles he did."

I then knew what the book was to be: I was to write about God's miracles in my life. I quickly jotted down one miracle after another. As I think about the miracles that God has covered me with, it is difficult for me to label them as such because I am fully aware that the leading of the Holy Spirit is what has brought them about. This leading has been a part of me since my conception! Yes, while I was still in the womb the Holy Spirit was working on my behalf.

I cannot tell about the miracles from God separate from telling about how the Holy Spirit works in us, around us, and through us. This does not in any way diminish the idea of miracles in my mind. After all, it seems to me, that the greatest miracle of all was God putting himself on a cross, dying in our place, so that he could have us with him forever. That's a Holy miracle.

So here, my children, I give you my story of THE POWER AND MIGHTY MIRACLES OF GOD.

Miracle of Birth

Psalm 71:6

"Yes, you have been with me from birth;

From my mother's womb you have cared for me.

No wonder I am always praising you!"

She was 24 years old, soon to be divorced twice from the same man, when she left him. It was another event in a long line of grief and pain for her. Orphaned at 16, raised by sisters barely older than she was, plagued by depression, she thought he was the love of her life. But only days after their first wedding she heard rumors that he was a cheat and a scoundrel.

As she fled to be cared for by her older sister, she believed that she not only had been betrayed again and again, but that she had an STD. She felt worthless and hopeless. A visit to the doctor should have brought her some relief when she learned that she was disease-free, but instead brought her a greater concern…she was pregnant.

Her former brother-in-law learned of her "predicament". It was 1951 and not only was divorce considered a sin, but to have a baby out of wedlock was degrading and a scandal. He and his wife picked up the young woman and took her to Dallas for dinner. It was only then that she learned that they had plans for her other than dinner. They had arranged for a doctor to perform an abortion, secreted away after hours.

The Holy Spirit intervened. She said, "No." Although she had no clue how she would make it through the days ahead, she knew that the child she was carrying was purposed by God and she needed that child to hold and to love.

I was that child. Born with a purpose, into love, into brokenness, into hope for my mother and myself. It was a miracle.

Miracle of Healing

[1]Proverbs 8:29

The LORD "gave the sea its boundaries so the waters would not overstep his command."

      I was a child who was always sick. I had cradle cap and was anemic. While I was small I had every childhood disease you can imagine: chicken pox, mumps, measles, whooping cough, scarlet fever. I had many ear infections, and to top it all off, I had one urinary tract infection (UTI) after another.

      In the 1950's my mother's family did not know how prevalent Polycystic Kidney Disease was within them, although they knew that Grandmother Deering had kidney disease and some of her daughters had signs of it. I was the first family member to be diagnosed as a child.

      The torture of kidney and UTI pain will bring down any adult, let alone a little child. It was my mother's faithful love and care that got me through it. Although I was only six years old, I remember in great detail being bribed to urinate, being promised ice cream after a painful clinic visit, holding my breath for x-ray after x-ray, putting my feet in the stirrups, and ultimately every step of being admitted to the Fort Worth Cook's Children's Hospital.

      The surgery to remove some of the cysts on my kidney was dangerous. Family members were put on stand-by to donate blood. As I waited in the iron-sided crib in my room, my mother's sister, Juanita taught me American Sign Language for the song *Jesus Loves Me*, and for the first time I felt the Holy Spirit fill the room as we sang and our hands signed together.

---

[1] I asked God to tell my kidney disease that it had boundaries and could only go so far, just as he tells the ocean to stay within its boundaries.

"Jesus loves me,

this I know

for the Bible tells me so.

Little ones to Him belong.

They are weak,

but he is strong."[2]

For sixty years following that delicate surgery, my kidneys functioned very well. That is a miracle.

---

[2] *Jesus Loves Me* by Anna Bartlett Warner

Miracle of Dreams

Genesis 31:11a (NIV)

"The angel of God said to me in a dream…"

When I was nine years old, I lived in an old two-story farm house in Crowley, Texas. The yard around the house contained nothing of specific interest with the exceptions of a gardenia bush, a ramshackle storm shelter, and a large old tree. I spent many hours in the yard playing, because my Daddy was a day-sleeper.

This year had been a turning-point for my life. My mother had remarried, we moved to Crowley, Texas to start a new life, and I left much of me behind.

One night I had a dream in which I went outside to the north side of the house, and there I saw a great chasm right in front of the big old tree. On the side where I stood was a brown teddy bear, while on the other side of the great divide was a wooden cross. A voice, that I presumed was God, said to me, "You must choose." How a nine year old could interpret what this scene meant, I do not know, but I was fully aware. I could make an easy choice and choose the bear, representing the things of the world, or I could choose the more difficult choice, the cross, representing a life of faith. I do not recall making a choice in my dream-state, but I do know that when I awoke, I had made my choice, the cross.

Later in life I had another dramatic dream. I was seated at a long wooden table that was full of people eating and enjoying themselves. I went to take a seat at the far side of the table, and I was redirected by someone (an angel?) to another room where there was a staircase. I stood at the bottom of the stairs and watched Jesus slowly descend toward me. I cannot describe him other than he had dark hair and was fully present. I began to bow before him and he told me to stand up and look. He held out his hands and said to me, "If you are to be one of my disciples, you must be willing to look at the scars in my hands." I took his hands in mine, rubbing my fingers across the nail prints and cried.

Like most people, I have had hundreds, even thousands of dreams in my life, but some I know instinctively are prophetic about my life. I have recorded many of them in my journals. I believe that God speaks to us through dreams, and my children can testify to this as well, having been gifted with their own dreams from God.

God speaking to us in our dreams is a miracle.

Miracle of Joining

Mark 10:9 (NIV)

"Therefore, what God has joined together, let no one separate."

In 1968 the Griffith family was ready to move from Missouri to Texas since Grandad Bob "Corky" had been transferred to General Dynamics in Fort Worth. Grandad and Grandma Dora "Debbie" had carefully selected a sight for their new home just south of Fort Worth, believing that the Fort Worth school district would be a good place to educate their five children. Their home was built in Hallmark, a subdivision of Fort Worth.

During the process of moving, Grandad and Grandma discovered that a little town further south, Crowley, had annexed Hallmark into their school district. The school was so small that 1968 would be the first year that they had a graduating class in Crowley, and it was 15 miles away from home.

I lived on a dairy farm in Crowley and was in the 10th grade. I never had a boyfriend and used to laughingly tell people, "I guess I will be the first Baptist nun." New students were coming to our school on a regular basis because of home building in and around Crowley. To me Ed was different from those students. I had never met anyone as smart as he was, and he was very friendly with the other girls in the class, always willing to listen to their drama. He always had a book in his hand or in his back pocket and I clumsily flirted with him, by stealing his pocket book from time-to-time. He didn't know that was flirting... how could he?

At the end of our sophomore year our class went on a trip to Six Flags Over Texas. On the bus ride there, my best friend Norma Cook and I sat in the seat in front of Steve Coolidge and his friend Ed. I turned around and began flirting hard with Ed, and as we arrived at the amusement park, I suggested that the four of us hang out together for the day. The boys agreed, and Norma was livid. She had no interest in hanging out with them. I spent all day making certain I stood close to Ed, sat by him on the rides, giggled at all his jokes. When it was time to return to the bus to head home, we walked side-by-side and I was thinking, "this is my last chance" as I bumped my hand up against his over and over, hoping he would eventually grab ahold. And he did just as we approached the bus. A great cheer came from our classmates as they watched the two of us walk up hand-in-hand.

On the bus ride home Ed put his arm around me and we heard Herman's Hermits sing *There's a Kind of Hush All Over the World.* This was the beginning of our courtship, which lasted on and off for the next two years. I have always believed that God moved Ed's family to Hallmark, and hence Crowley School District, joining Ed and I forever. On December 8, 1971 we were married. Ed has often told me that he hopes we both die at the same instant because he can't go a day without me! That kind of love is a miracle!

Miracle of Adoption

Psalm 68:6 (NLT)

"God places the lonely in families…"

When I was in Junior High, my Sunday School teacher was Mrs. Peggy Duvall. Peggy had a passion for orphans, and she drew me into her passion. We regularly would visit the Lena Pope Home, a Baptist orphanage in Fort Worth, where I began to see the plight of the children without parents to care for them, as my mother had done for me.

Eventually Peggy adopted two sons from that institution. God kept me engaged with the passion for orphans, even into college, when my friend Marilyn "Hope" Hawk invited me to volunteer at a Catholic Foster Home/Orphanage. Ed and I were dating at the time and he came along as a volunteer, seeing for himself children in need of love and attention.

After Ed and I were married we were blessed with our sons, Eddy and Zach. I made the decision after Zach's birth to not have any more children, but to wait and adopt other children.

In the spring of 1982, I began having dreams about adoption, several in a row. In one dream a little girl with a crutch stood in front of a table laden with food. She was crying because she couldn't get to the food. This dream really stirred my heart. But only one dream left me with the desire to take action. In this dream, I walked out of our apartment in LaHabra, California (where we lived at that time) and greeted a young woman who stood with two little girls. She was so young, I thought that the three were sisters, but I soon realized that she was their young mother. I asked her, "Are they the ones?" She nodded. One little girl was chunky and robust and hopping around her birth mother. The other child was frail and hiding behind her mother. I took the two little ones by the hand and led them back across the street toward our apartment.

About the time of this dream, Ed was doing a job search. He was hired by the University of Texas at El Paso. We moved the family that summer. In December 1982 Ed and I attended an adoption information meeting for the Foster Care System in El Paso, Texas. On December 8 (our 11th wedding anniversary) we went to Red Lobster to celebrate our love and filled out our adoption application. We put serious thought into the process and ended up stating that we wanted sisters less than 6 years of age.

After mailing in our application, Ed called the adoption office every month, asking how long before we could have our children. One year later, December 1983, he was given a long-awaited answer, "Yes, we have children becoming available that meet your profile." We began a six-week adoption training class with about 12 other couples in February 1984.

During the third week of the training we were having a group discussion about our extended families and Ed had the floor. He was telling the details of his mother's large family, noting specifically that there were three sets of twins. During the break a case worker, Rosario, asked us to step into her office. She said that after hearing Ed's story about the twins in his family she thought that we might be a match for two little girls, twins. I asked her, "What's wrong with them?" She replied that they were "not yet two and Anglo. All that is wrong is they need a good home." She then explained to us that there was urgency in getting them placed because they were separated in foster care and she felt they needed to be reunited. Therefore, if we agreed to take the girls, we would have to rush through the process, and they would be placed with us as soon as the six-week class was complete. We said "yes". We had just three weeks to get our adoption physicals, home visits, and many other things accomplished. Rosario instructed us to make life books for each of the girls, with family info and photos, so the foster families could begin preparing the children for their move. She also instructed us to get some sort of gifts to present to the girls when we met them for the first time, to help us bond with them.

Ed knew right away what gifts he wanted to find – cloth dolls. We looked at the toy stores in El Paso and found nothing that fitted his image of what the gifts should be. We took a trip to Las Cruces to check out the toy store there. On that trip we dreamed about life with our new daughters and what that would look like. We giggled as we chatted about names. Rosario had told us that we could change their names if we wished. We knew twins who were adopted named Minnie and Winnie Grubbs, and laughed about those names. I said, "I hope they aren't rhyming names like Julie and July. I think names more like Amanda and Samantha would be cute." I had no idea what I was saying.

At the Las Cruces Mall Ed found just what he was looking for, two little cloth dolls with aprons. One had "Amanda" embroidered on the apron, the other was blank. He was concerned that a name was on one and not the other, but decided that was the right choice, so we made the purchases and headed home.

We took all the steps necessary and on the last day of class, Rosario announced to the group that we would be the first couple to have children placed with us, and then gave us photographs of the girls that were taken on December 19, 1983 (my birthday). Rosario announced that the girls were named… Amanda and Samantha. I was amazed! My next thought was, "Oh no! We have an "Amanda" doll, but the other doll doesn't have a name.

I was a Cub Scout leader, along with Marian Daross.   A couple of days after my realization that I needed a doll labeled "Samantha", I was at Marian's and shared my dilemma. She told me she had a friend that could do machine embroidery and she thought that her friend would love to help me out. She made a quick phone call and I headed out the door to the seamstress. As she added the name "Samantha" on the doll's apron, I told her the story about how I knew their names before we were told and our adoption plans. She mentioned that her husband practiced family law and she thought he might be able to help us. I was still at her house visiting when he arrived, and she had me retell my story to him. He agreed to represent us for the adoption and stated that he would give us two for the price of one. As an aside, this couple had twin four-year-old daughters, and they gifted us with beautiful clothes that their girls had outgrown.

Shortly after this we went to get Samantha, and then two days later, brought Amanda home. When I saw them both playing at the park the day we had them together for the first time, I realized they were the children in my dream. I now knew their birth mother was only 17 when they were born. Samantha was frail and shy, while Amanda was indeed robust and outgoing.

God's plan for this adoption was a miracle that He grew in me over a 20-year period, and it's ongoing. I'm still amazed.

Miracle of Protection

Psalm 89:18 (NLT)

"Yes, our protection comes from the LORD… "

In the 1990's while watching the TV sitcom *Third Rock From the Sun*, I heard one of the characters say, "Sometimes on the way to something you find something else." I wrote this down and it lives in my brain to this day, 20 years later.

We were "on our way" to adopting our daughters in February 1984. Part of the process was for Ed and I to each get a physical. I expected a clean bill of health, but to my surprise that wasn't the case. I hadn't had a PAP smear in years, and this one revealed the beginning signs of cancer (cervical dysplasia). When I heard the news, I was fear-filled, and wondered what the future would hold for my family with this new development. My doctor arranged for me to have a type of surgery where they freeze the diseased tissue off the cervix. I had normal PAP smears from then on.

I often wondered, "What if God had not led us down this path of adoption? Would this have been discovered too late to take care of it." God protected my life through the process of adopting our daughters, and that is a miracle.

*****

I had been suffering with pain in my left hip for months in 2004-2005. I had seen all kinds of doctors, had tests run, and received treatments. Nothing seemed to help. I ended up at a pain management clinic, and the doctor suggested that I get an MRI so that he could get a better look. I hadn't had an MRI before and didn't know what to expect. I changed into a gown and was escorted into a room with a giant white tube with a bed sticking out of it like a tongue. The technologist helped me up onto the bed, taped my feet together, and handed me a button to press in case I needed help. Then she placed headphones on my ears and piped in music. The bed slowly slid into the tube and the loud click, click, clacking began. It wasn't too bad after all.

Quite a few minutes later the noise stopped, and the bed emerged once again from the machine. The technician said, "Good job. Did you know that you have Polycystic Kidney Disease (PKD)?" No, I didn't. Kidney disease was prevalent in my family, that I knew. As a child I had what was described to me as "two benign tumors" removed from my left kidney, and my mother had suffered many years from cysts on her kidneys that ruptured. I knew nothing about PKD and never was diagnosed with that as far as I knew.

I went home and did online research and found out that 1) there is no cure for PKD; 2) PKD patients eventually go on dialysis or need a transplant; 3) cerebral aneurysms are common among people with PKD; and 4) at that time, PKD patients were uninsurable. I knew that momma's mother, Hattie Deering, had kidney disease and that my mother had it as well, but I never knew it was PKD. My mother and two of her sisters, Laura and Vernon had all died of cerebral aneurysms. Through research I eventually discovered that all the girls in momma's family had died of kidney disease, or complications of the disease such as stroke or aneurysm.

Once again, I was on the way to something – relief from hip pain – when something else happened, PKD. I found a nephrologist and began keeping a regular schedule of visits. I believe that this "something else" that I learned about miraculously prolonged my kidney health for the next ten years.

*****

My kidneys failed in 2016 and I began dialysis in September of that year. Right away my care team asked me if I was planning on getting a kidney transplant. I didn't have to think twice about this and asked for an application. As I completed the mound of paperwork required, I felt an urgency that I shouldn't waste any time. I believed that I felt this because God had a kidney donor planned for me.

Not only were there lots of questions to answer, but there were things to be done. I needed to prove that other than my kidneys I was in good health. Of all the testing that I needed to have done, the one thing that truly frightened me was getting a good report from a dentist. I hated going to the dentist! I had a traumatic, painful time with a dentist when I was in high school, and from then on getting me to go to a dentist, even when I was in pain, was like "pulling teeth" (excuse the pun!). Ed thought that his dentist was very good and encouraged me as I made an appointment. I found out later that he had actually called the dentist's office and told them about my fears so that they would treat me gently. He even had arranged for me to have a hand massage to relax me, while they were working in my mouth. My whole experience was wonderful. Dr. John Werner was kind and patient. Since I had avoided going to the dentist for years, it took several visits for me to get caught up on cleanings, fillings, and crowns.

Dr. Emily Todd, my primary doctor, set up appointments for a mammogram and colonoscopy. With dental work pretty much behind me, the day I went in for my mammogram I felt like I was truly "on my way" to getting a transplant. After the pictures were taken, the radiology technologist asked me to wait for a few minutes. When she came back in the room, she called me over to her computer to show me the mammogram results. There was a tiny spider-like place in my left breast. She told me that she had consulted the radiologist and he was free right then to do a needle biopsy. I agreed because this was something that I didn't want drug out over time since I was getting ready for my transplant.

The radiologist told me that he was 90% certain that this was a cyst cluster. I felt relieved. I went home and waited for the results. Two days later Dr. Todd called me. She said, "Karen I have the results of the biopsy and it is as we expected." What I expected was that it was a cyst cluster just as the radiologist had said, so I breathed a sigh of relief. She continued, "It's cancer." I stood quietly and heard her say other things which I would not be able to recall. All that came to my mind was that I would be ineligible for a transplant. I was heartsick.

When I got over the shock of the news, I realized that once again God had provided a means for the discovery of this tiny cancer and saved my life. If it were not for kidney failure, plan to transplant, and this mammogram, I could have died. Once again I was on the way to something when something else was discovered.

I had a lumpectomy in March of 2017 and four weeks of radiation in the summer. In January of 2018 I was declared cancer-free! There is a five year wait after breast cancer to be eligible for the transplant program. I don't know in five years what God will lead me to, but I think you'll agree that this was a miraculous way for God to show his love for me.

Miracle of Seeking and Finding

Matthew 7:7 (NIV)

"Ask and it will be given to you; seek and you will find; knock and the door will be opened to you."

When I was a senior in high school (1970) I was snooping through my mother's dresser drawers where I knew her to keep secret things. It wasn't my first snoop through those treasure boxes, and I was looking for something specific on this occasion, envelopes bundled together with brittle rubber bands. I thumbed through the stack and found a letter from the Social Security Administration which explained who the recipients were for monthly benefits being distributed because my birth father was disabled.

I had been estranged from the Erwin family since my mother had remarried my dear step-daddy in 1961. I knew nothing of my father, having not seen him since I was 9 years old, so the news of his disability brought all kinds of questions to my mind. As I read through the document my heart raced. I was quite surprised to learn that my birth father had two other children, sons. Oh, how I wanted to run to my momma and ask her to validate what I had read, but I couldn't do that since it was information I had gained by violating her privacy. So, I held the idea of these two brothers in my heart and in my mind.

In 1992 my family moved to Mustang, Oklahoma. As we traveled northward on I-35 I saw the sign for the turn to Ada, and my heart jumped. Ada was the hometown of my mother's family, the Deering's, as well as my father's family, the Erwin's. I thought to myself, "Now that we're here, I'll try to find my Erwin family." Shortly after we settled into our new home, I made a visit to the Oklahoma City Public Library, specifically to look at an Ada phone book. I found four Erwin families listed. They all had phone numbers, of course, but I was leery and didn't want to make a call. Only two had addresses good enough for mailing a letter. On

July 26 I wrote to the two families and explained that I was searching for my family. I never heard from them.

After settling into our new home, I secured a job with the Eldercare Access Center and was sent to a seminar at East Central University in Ada. On August 25, for almost 100 miles, I drove toward Ada feeling like I was a chunk of steel and Ada was a giant magnet drawing me rapidly toward it. I couldn't shake the notion that I was predestined to make the journey. I remember nothing about the seminar, but I do recall sitting there wondering where I could go in Ada to find a missing link that would connect me with the Erwin family. At the conclusion of the seminar I asked some of the presenters if they knew of a historical society in Ada. There was one! I was on my way.

At the Historical Society I saw many photos of Ada in the "good old days" (as my mother used to say), but the curator told me I'd have better luck looking for family information at the Genealogical Society and directed me there. I walked into the converted house and was greeted by a little old lady. I blurted out, "I know most people come here looking for dead relatives, but I'm looking for some that I hope are still alive."

The curator spent two hours with me looking through microfiche records. During this time, we discovered that my mother had married and divorced my father not once, but twice. I also found my father's death certificate, but nothing to lead me to living family members. I left the Genealogical Society and began to make my way through town to return home. I had a strong feeling that I shouldn't leave without doing something, but what? I spotted the office of the *Ada Evening News*. "That's it," I thought. "I'll run an ad." I walked up to the counter of the little newspaper office and was asked by the clerk, "May I help you?" It was easy to reply, "I want to run a personal ad." Now what I was thinking was something big, in bold type, maybe even colored print, with flashing neon lights as the border – something that no Erwin would miss.

The clerk continued, "What would you like your ad to say?" What a loaded question. The clerk had no clue how I was standing at the crossroads of changing my life – neither did I. The thought ran through my mind that I had to protect my family. Very carefully I began to write on the little slip of paper that the clerk handed me:

"Searching for family members of George A. Erwin.

Call Karen Erwin Griffith. (405) 946-3388."

I held my breath as I wrote and gave my office phone number. The clerk then asked me if I would like to have a copy of the paper mailed to my home. I enthusiastically responded, "Yes!" My total bill was exactly the amount of money I had left in my purse. I sighed a satisfactory sigh, got in my car and headed home. It was a week later before the paper arrived. Searching through several pages of ads, I came upon mine. I was so disappointed. I had no faith that such a tiny little ad would be seen by anyone.

It was Friday, October 9, 1992 when I came back to my office from lunch, that my life's course changed. I will always remember it was a Friday because earlier that week I had eaten Chinese food, and my fortune cookie slip read, "Good news comes on a Friday." The office receptionist matter-of-factly said, "You have a long-distance phone call from a Woodrow Erwin of Taos, New Mexico."

My feet could not run fast enough the few steps to reach the phone on my desk. I answered, "Hello." The very familiar and often longed for voice of my father's brother, Woodrow Erwin, spoke into my ear, "Is this Karen Erwin Griffith?" I replied, "Yes, it is." He continued, "Is this the Karen Erwin that used to live around Fort Worth, Texas?" I replied, "Yes, it is." He asked, "Do you know who this is?" I confirmed, "You are my Uncle Woody." Tears of joy leaked from my eyes! It seemed too good to be true. Woodrow Erwin was my Father's older brother. Uncle Woody had been a big part of my life until Momma remarried when I was nine. I hadn't seen him for 31 years.

Uncle Woody told me the story of how that tiny little ad made its way to him:

"About four weeks ago our Cuz Lee Daggs, Jr, who is the son of Daddy's oldest sister (whom we called Big Aunty), who lives in Ada, wrote me a letter, and sent me a tiny, tiny clipping out of the ads of the *Ada Evening News*. Lee wrote that our Cuz R.H. Erwin (Daddy's brother, Uncle Rit's son) called him on the phone and told him about seeing the ad in the paper – a very unlikely happen-in-stance, no doubt. Lee dug out the paper, found the ad and mailed it to me."

In a letter to the Erwin family Woody continued the story:

"I immediately called the number in the ad which proved to be her workplace, and being on a weekend, I didn't get Karen but a phone recorded message. Later next week I called and we made contact, hallelujah! Then the scenario unraveled most rapidly with me telling her a little about myself and very much about her two brothers and their mother Mary, giving her addresses and phone numbers. I'm greatly touched and overjoyed and deeply grateful to Our good Lord for bothering to dip His Fingers in all this and help bring it about."

Suddenly I had two new brothers. I had spent twenty-two years, a life-time, longing for them and then there they were. Uncle Woody contacted Mary who contacted George and Steve. The next day, October 10, 1992, I heard their voices for the first time. They told me they had always known about me. They had pictures of me passed along to my Father from my mother's sister Alma that were kept in their family Bible. Steve said that he would go to look at the pictures from time-to-time and dream of what his life would be like if I was in it.

Within days I was on a plane to Fort Smith, Arkansas to meet my brothers. From that time on the three of us, and all our spouses and kids, experienced many firsts: first hugs, first family meetings, first Christmas, first vacation together, first trip to Raymondville, Texas where I met my Father's sister Ruth and her family, meeting my Father's sister Mary Kate, first reunion with

Uncle Woody, first laughter, first shared tears, first gifts, first songs, first chapter for a long-awaited love story.

Years later, I learned that at the same time God was drawing me to George and Steve, Steve had been writing letters and trying to find me. Uncle Woody was correct; indeed, the good Lord dipped his finger in all of this, and that is a miracle.

*****

On January 31, 1997 George died from cardiac failure, only 4 years, 3 months, and 21 days from the first time we spoke. He would have been 43 on June 11 of that year. If I had not responded to the Holy Spirit's leading and timing, I might have missed knowing him at all. I was devastated when he died. After the funeral, as I was leaving Roland, Oklahoma where he made his home, at the end of the road was a little church with this sign: "Love is measured in deeds, not in years."

Miracle of Intervention

Hebrews 1:14 (NIV)

"Are not all angels ministering spirits sent to serve those who will inherit salvation?"

When I read through my journal entries of 1996 and 1997, time and time again I wrote messages to God asking Him to send angels to protect my son, Zach. And God indeed did just that. At the age of 20, Zach was lost, making poor decisions, and at odds with his dad and I. There was much going on in our lives with chaos all around us, and I felt hopeless as I watched my loving son transform into a person that I didn't know. I made hard decisions on how to love him through this. And I always prayed.

In December Zach was deep in darkness. I received a phone call that he was in a safe place for the holidays and that put my mind somewhat at ease. Zach recalls that one day he left Oklahoma City with nothing except his boots without laces and his pants, no shirt. Our home was 17 miles away, and he started walking until he was in a rural area. A woman in a late model car, wearing a business suit, stopped to inquire if he needed help. He told her he was trying to get home. He directed her to our home in Mustang.

Ed and I were at work when his rescuer pulled up in front of our house. Our neighbor, Bonnie Franklin, was in her front yard watching her children play. The woman asked, "Do you know this young man?" Bonnie confirmed that he was her neighbor's son. The woman asked if Zach would be safe if she left him there, and Bonnie said she would call Ed and I and let us know.

This was his first angel. How do I know? What business woman on this planet would stop in the middle of nowhere Oklahoma and pick up a bedraggled young man and take him home? I believe God answered my prayers for angels through her.

Zach told me that some time after this he was hanging out in Norman, Oklahoma when a young man came up to him and asked him for a cigarette. Zach gave him one. The man asked Zach, "What are you doing here? You don't belong here." Zach never saw him again. This was his second angel. How do I know? Because of this young man's message to Zach he began to take steps that would eventually lead to him getting the help that he needed. I believe God answered my prayers for angels through that young man.

The story doesn't end here.   Zach moved to Iowa with his brother Eddy in the spring of 1997 for a fresh start. On many occasions he has given a testimony of how angels led him back home and back to the life he was purposed for. He knows what God did for him and lives a life that reflects that.

"There are only two ways to live your life.

One is as though nothing is a miracle.

The other is as though everything is a miracle."

-- Albert Einstein

God's intervention to save Zach's life was a miracle.

Miracle of Brotherly Love

Psalm 133:1a (KJV)

"Behold, how good and how pleasant it is for brothers to dwell together in unity!"

Before my second son was born I had hoped that he and his older brother would be close. I was so close to my own brother, Max, that I wanted nothing less for my children. At first Eddy was excited at the prospect of a new brother, but he was highly disappointed that the kid that we brought home was not what he expected; he was definitely not someone to play with.

In the first moments with the two of them together, Eddy stood fascinated as I laid his brother Zach down on the changing table. Then Zach pee'd all over him! Eddy stood aghast that this kid had defiled him. I don't know if he ever got over it! (LOL) Eddy did make attempts to befriend this less than expected newcomer. He threw metal trucks into Zach's crib for him to play with, and he tried holding him for short moments.

As they grew, I was disappointed to see that they weren't close. They fought. They challenged. They resented. It wasn't a pretty picture. And through it all, I prayed for them to be close brothers.

In 1997, Zach was going through some hard times, very hard times. I didn't know how to pray any longer. I didn't know what the future would hold for him, or how to help him. He was at our home in Yukon, Oklahoma on Easter Sunday for a visit when the phone rang. It was Eddy. He was calling from his home in Iowa. I expected this call because we usually had a phone visit on special occasions and holidays. I was stunned, however, when he asked to speak with Zach.

I put Zach on the phone and eavesdropped and wondered what Eddy was up to. It didn't take long for Zach's dreary eyes to pop open, and his entire countenance to change. Eddy was calling to give Zach the hope that he needed. He said, "Come live with me. I'll get you a job where I work, and we'll get you through this." Our whole household lit up with the news as we celebrated not only our Lord's resurrection that day, but the resurrection of the love between brothers.

Within days Zach was on a plane to Iowa. I don't think I even thanked Eddy for doing this, but I thanked God over and over again for this gesture from brother to brother. There were some ups and downs over the next few months, but in my eyes, it did not diminish the significance of this change in their relationship.

I love both of my sons more than they'll ever know, and the fact that they could come together and demonstrate love to each other is truly a miracle.

Miracle of Visions

1 Kings 19:11b-13 (NIV)

"...a great and powerful wind tore the mountains apart and shattered the rocks before the LORD, but the LORD was not in the wind. After the wind there was an earthquake, but the LORD was not in the earthquake. After the earthquake came a fire, but the LORD was not in the fire. And after the fire came a gentle whisper."

There have been periods in my life when prayer and fellow believers were all that sustained me. I can only surmise that the visions that I'm going to share here were the result of such "praying without ceasing"[3] seasons.

On an ordinary day in the mid-1990s I went to a worship service at St. Luke's United Methodist Church (Oklahoma City) to hear Rev. Dave Poteet preach. The service was in the small chapel rather than the sanctuary. I don't have any idea what the topic was or that the message was particularly meaningful to me. I just looked up and saw angels.

Behind Dave as he spoke were several brighter than the sun figures that were not static but constantly in movement. I closed my eyes and reopened them several times to refresh my vision and my thinking. It was surreal. There were no features that would distinguish them as angels as these heavenly beings have been portrayed ... no wings, no halos, not a single harp. They were just there, surrounding Dave and moving as if they were attending to him only.

I have never seen this vision again, but ever since that day, from time to time, when I'm in worship, I have seen the same heavenly bright light surround speakers or musicians, and have come to believe it is the presence of the Holy Spirit. I cannot

---

[3] 1 Thessalonians 5:17

conjure it up; it just happens. I simply thank God for this incredible sign of his Holy presence.

*****

Another vision that God gave to me was of a different nature. It was around the year 2000 and my family was in pieces. Ed and I had broken relationships with my brother, Max and my children, and they had broken relationships with each other. Again, this was a time of much grieving and praying. One day as I sat at my desk in our home in Cleburne, Texas, I felt God's prompting in my spirit. I felt I was being instructed to go outside and pick up seven sticks. No one was home to see me, so I thought, "Why not?" I picked up seven sticks each about 7" long, dropped down from the big old pecan tree in our back yard. I took them in the house and laid them on the desk and waited a bit. Nothing happened.

I wondered, "Why seven?" I knew the number 7 represented completeness in the Bible and thought that must be why I picked up that number. The next day, as I sat at the desk and looked at the pile of twigs, again I felt God prompt my spirit to go outside and pick up seven sticks. I began to think I was nuts but did it anyway. I brought them back into my study area and heard[4] God say, "Now break these seven". As I broke them one-by-one, I realized there was one for myself, one for Ed, one for Max, one for Eddy, one for Zach, one for Amanda, and one for Samantha. God revealed to me that the broken sticks represented the broken relationships in our family that I had been praying so hard about.

Then God told me to bind the unbroken sticks together because he was going to mend all our relationships and bind us all together with His love. I was so happy to receive this promise! I drove quickly to the store and bought a picture frame and golden cord and came back and created a memorial to the message. I placed the seven broken sticks within the frame, tied the whole ones with the gold cord and made a label that read: "Bind us

---

[4] When I say "heard" or "hear" from God, it's not a voice. It's an impression on my mind, heart, or spirit that comes from nowhere, with a message that I'm certain doesn't originate with me.

together Lord, with cords that cannot be broken."[5] I hung it on the wall near my study. I told Zach about my vision and from time-to-time he would ask me if my sticks were still broken. Over the years they have all been restored except one... it will be someday.

There's more to this story. When I was a pastor, one Sunday God led me to preach on forgiveness. I gave everyone a twig that I had hand-picked from our yard in Cleburne. I told them to think about the person that they had a broken relationship with and to let their stick represent that broken relationship. Then I told them to break those sticks. The weeping was great as the Holy Spirit swept through the room, as the people broke their twigs. I instructed them to bring them to the communion table and lay them down before God. The procession of believers with broken sticks was a beautiful sight.

I collected all the pieces and over the next week two-by-two, made little crosses from them. The next Sunday I gave them back to the people as a demonstration of God's promise to heal their broken relationships. They were amazed. This wasn't from me! This was God working through me.

*****

One day I was busy transferring books from one room in my house to another. I had been gifted with many theological volumes by a member of my church, Stella Mooring. Stella's husband had been a United Methodist Minister and had recently passed away. As I moved one pile of books after another, I became tired and exasperated. I picked up another pile and as I did, one of my fingernails broke down into the quick. I carried the load toward the bookshelf and sat in front of it, feeling sorry for myself, trying not to cry. I picked up a hymnal that had belonged to Dr. Mooring and saw something sticking up between the pages. I opened it to find an emery board! My mouth dropped open! As I picked it up and began to file my broken nail, I looked down at the page of the hymn

---

[5] Lyrics to *Bind Us Together* by Bob Gillman (an old familiar hymn)

book and saw these words, "Be not dismayed whatever betide. God will take care of you."[6]

Sometimes miracles are supernatural and unexplainable. I have been asked why I can experience such things when others cannot. I have no answer. I do know that I look for God in my life. I do not believe in coincidences. I believe that God works in, through, and all around me to demonstrate His love for me.

---

[6] "God will Take Care of You" by Civilla Martin

Miracle of Call to Ministry

Jeremiah 3:15 (NIV)

"Then I will give you shepherds after my own heart, who will lead you with knowledge and understanding."

When I was 14 years old, I was a very active member of the Crowley First Baptist Church. I was beginning to discern the Holy Spirit moving in my life from time-to-time. One Wednesday evening I was at the mid-week prayer service without my parents. I don't remember how I got there or what the teaching was about. I don't even recall who the pastor was. At the end of the service the Holy Spirit began to speak to my heart. I didn't ignore it. Soon the service was closing and I was walking forward to speak to the pastor. I told him I believed that God was calling me to be a foreign missionary. The pastor affirmed my calling and the congregation joyfully surrounded me. I had no doubt about what I was saying or committing to.

When I returned home my mother was already in bed. I went into her bedroom and she asked me how the evening went. I told her that I had dedicated my life to foreign missions. She blew up! She was angry over my being "too young to know your own mind". The last thing I wanted to do was disappoint my mother, so I shelved the whole idea and never spoke of it again.

*****

In September 1996, at the age of 44, I started a class called *Becoming Disciples Through Bible Study*. The lesson for the second week was about Creation and I wrote in my workbook, "God, if you can bring order to the chaos of nothingness, please bring order to the chaos of my life." I was a daughter of Eve and liked to be in control. Every day I went to the orchard to pick another apple, while trying to be obedient to God. So there was conflict between the will of God and my own, and I knew it. If I had been sitting with

Dr. Phil, rather than with 11 other Bible students, I'm certain he would have asked me, "How's that working for you?"

Well, that prayer was my surrender and the next nine months were traumatic and difficult as any time I have ever faced. Chaos was all around us and revealed itself steadily. Each week as I sat in the Bible class, telling the others about the next chapter of chaos, they sat in disbelief, and I sat in gratefulness, that God provided this network of believers to help me survive.

From September 1996 to June 1997 these events unfolded:

Ed went to the emergency room with a hiatal hernia.

Ed's dad had congestive heart failure.

My daughter Amanda left a note in my calendar that she was expecting. She was 14 years old and 8 months pregnant.

Our beloved family dog injured her back.

My brother George died suddenly from a heart attack.

My son Zach, just 20 years old, was making poor decisions that impacted our whole family.

Amanda's baby was born, our second grandchild, and she gave him up for adoption.

Our landlord gave us a 30 day notice that he wanted to relocate to our home, and we had to find a house to buy and move.

I had a major anxiety attack and was admitted to the hospital because it mimicked a heart attack.

I quit my job.

A routine mammogram revealed a lump in my breast.

Ed's pupils became unequal and one was non-reactive, making us think he had a stroke.

Although it didn't feel like it at the time, in the midst of all of this, there was God, taking control and reordering our lives. Not only did my classmates from the Bible class support me, but God sent people from many directions to shore us up in the storm. One such person was Dr. Jim Pertree, our family chiropractor. At one of my appointments he saw my downcast countenance and asked about my spiritual health. I gave him a briefing on the drama/trauma I was attempting to survive. He told me, "Karen, I want you to go home and sit down and thank God for every single one of those events. You won't know why you are thanking him, but the Bible says to give thanksgiving in everything." I was desperate and willing to try anything. I went home and sat with my journal, and through my wailing and sobbing, thanked God one-by-one for the events that I was attempting to understand.

During the summer I was in what I have come to call a desert time. I was deeply depressed and drained. All I could manage to do was to sit outside among the beautiful flowers that surrounded our new home. One day, when I was deadheading zinnias, I spoke out a prayer for God to send me a friend. He sent me Cheryl Smith who was one of the members of my Bible class. Cheryl called me and told me that she was offered a job that she couldn't accept and thought I might be interested. I took that job, and there found another friend, Barbara Allen-Rosser, a pink Cadillac-driving Mary Kay director. I went to work for Barbara as a "girl Friday"[7], and through the simple tasks of a servant and Barbara's friendship, began to heal.

At our church, St. Luke's United Methodist in Oklahoma City, I would often read in the church bulletin of meetings of Emmaus Reunion groups. I asked the youth pastor, Anne King, what those groups were, and she explained to me that they were meetings of people who had attended *The Walk to Emmaus*. She

---

[7] "In the novel Robinson Crusoe, Crusoe had a man he called *Friday* as his helper. *Friday* did just about anything Crusoe asked him to do. *Girl Friday* is a reference to a female worker who can and will do just about any sort of work her boss demands, just as the man *Friday* did for Crusoe." www.answers.com

asked me if she could sponsor me to attend a walk. I said, "yes" although I had no idea what to expect because she was tight-lipped about the details.

In October 1997, I was leaving work to head to the Walk to Emmaus and went into Barbara's office to tell her goodbye. I said, "Barbara, I have a strong feeling that God is going to reveal something to me this weekend." Without missing a beat, Barbara came back with, "I think I know what it is." "What?" I asked. With a glint in her eye, Barbara stated emphatically, "I think he's going to ask you to sell Mary Kay!" All I could say, was "Okay," because I knew there had to be more to it than that. (This still makes me chuckle.)

Anne took me to St. Mark's United Methodist Church on that Thursday evening and left me there with my Bible, which she left on my bed opened to the scripture Luke 24:13-35, *On the Emmaus Road*. This was a three-day weekend with women of all faiths, where we heard 15 talks from lay people as well as clergy, taking a spiritual walk with Christ Jesus as the scriptures were explained to us. That evening we were instructed to go to bed in silence and not speak until after communion the next morning.

On Friday morning as I took communion, I said this prayer, "God, I feel like I've been a caterpillar in a cocoon. Am I ready to come out and be a butterfly?" From there we went to breakfast and I sat at a random place and waited to be served. A woman came by laying a cloth book-jacket at every place for our Emmaus worship books. At my place she laid one down that was pink and covered with BUTTERFLIES! I looked around me and no one else had butterflies on theirs. I knew this was my answer.

The first talk was on priorities. The speaker concluded with "just say yes". I wondered what I was supposed to say yes to. The second talk was on grace, and how God draws us to himself. I felt I was being drawn to him. Throughout the day, I felt this compelling longing to say "yes" but I didn't know what the question was.

Saturday, on the way to a special prayer service, I spotted a picture hanging in the hallway of Jesus holding a little lamb. The look on Jesus' face as he looked at the lamb in his arms, shone with pure love. I thought to myself, "Jesus, am I that lamb?" After the time of prayer, we were told to scatter throughout the sanctuary to spend some alone time with God. I found a spot near a pillar that felt isolated. I took off my sweatshirt, put it on the back of the pew in front of me and bent over, placing my head on the shirt. I prayed, "God, am I your little lamb?" I immediately heard, "Yes, I am giving you a flock." I sat straight up! I looked around to see if anyone was there. I reluctantly put my head back down. "Jesus," I began, "are you asking what I think you're asking?" I heard the reply, "Just say 'yes'". I continued the conversation in my head. "Don't ask that of me! I'll volunteer anywhere you want me to, but a pastor? Please don't ask that of me." Jesus said, "From everyone who has been given much, much will be expected."[8] I sat up and squirmed in my chair. I whispered, "yes". I looked to the right behind the pillar and there was a beautiful stained-glass window depicting Jesus as the shepherd with his sheep. I felt affirmation. Then I heard Jesus say, "I anoint you to pastor my sheep." I didn't tell anyone.

Sunday morning, I had a question for Jesus, "What about Ed?" After all we had been through in the last year, if I came to him and told him I was being called to be a pastor, he might think I had finally lost my mind! So I began seeking out the clergy at the Walk, and asked each about their spouse's response to their being in ministry. None of their answers satisfied me. By Sunday afternoon I was in a tizzy and feeling ill about the idea of telling Ed. Then God spoke, "Don't worry about Ed. He doesn't express his feelings easily, as you know. You don't really know what he will think, or what his relationship is with me. I gave Ed to you in a covenant of marriage. I will not allow you to lose him because you are being faithful to me." That settled it. I felt at peace.

Sunday evening there was a closing ceremony, and each participant was given the time to say what the Walk had meant to them and what they were going to do with their experience. I stood up proudly and announced that I was answering a call to go into the

---

[8] Luke 12:48b

ministry. A girl standing next to me questioned me, "You're going to seminary?" I was dumbfounded! That had not crossed my mind.

Anne returned to collect me and on the way home I couldn't get the words out quick enough to share my story of my time with Jesus and how he was calling me to be a pastor. Anne received the news with joy! When I got home I was glad to see Ed but resolved not to say a word to him about my weekend. I couldn't keep it in. We sat at our dining table and I shared what I could about the talks and such, but then it came out of my mouth, "I believe Jesus wants me to be a pastor." I waited. I will never forget Ed's body language. He had been leaning forward, listening intently, but when those words left my mouth, he sat back, crossed his legs and arms and replied, "I'm not surprised. After all, you are who you are." I pointed out that as United Methodists we might have to move in order for me to serve. He assured me and replied, "You have followed me all over the U.S. for 25 years. It's my turn to follow you."

Soon after, I became a candidate for pastor in the United Methodist Church. During this process over the span of four years, I was asked to think about what type of church I pictured myself pastoring in the next five years. My answer was either a church with elderly people that was small and needed to be revitalized, or a church with mixed racial groups who needed leadership in becoming one body. My first appointment was a dual charge in the Corsicana District. The two churches I served were exactly as I had described.

The miracles on my road to ministry were many, but I know the biggest miracle of all was that God chose me, although I was among "the least, the last and the lost,"[9] to love his sheep and lead them. I represented the mother of a pregnant teen, the sister of a brother who died too young, the mother of a mentally ill son, and yes, Eve, and God has used every single hurt in my life to help me come alongside others and point them to Jesus.

---

[9] Disciple Bible Study description of those God calls and uses.

Miracle of Saint Francis

"The tree of love its roots hath spread

Deep in my heart, and rears its head;

Rich are its fruits: they joy dispense;

Transport the heart, and ravish sense.

In love's sweet swoon to thee I cleave,

Bless'd source of love."

Francis of Assisi

In 1998 I was recovering from a very difficult couple of years and had recently been called to become a candidate for pastor in the United Methodist Church. I urgently needed to get away and spend some time with myself and my Lord. I remembered that the year before a good friend had given me a prayer guide that she picked up at a retreat center in Oklahoma. I dug it out of my book box to find the contact information for that center.

The center was Saint Francis of the Woods in Coyle, Oklahoma. It took only about one and one-half hours to make the drive from my home. I stopped at a Walmart along the way and picked up supplies, including foods that would not only refresh me, but that I seldom would buy just for myself. When I arrived at the camp I was surprised that the caretaker had reserved a whole cabin for me. It was simply decorated with books and pictures that all pointed to Jesus. There was a sitting area and two bedrooms and a bath, plus a screened-in porch with Adirondack chairs.

I unpacked the items I had brought for the weekend including lots of CD's with my favorite praise music, my Bible, journal and other books. I sat on the porch and enjoyed a cool breeze and prayed thanksgiving prayers. I decided to go explore the grounds. Nearby was a prayer garden. It was ecumenical with symbols and signs from many faiths. I walked through respectfully taking it all in.

As I continued walking I spotted a library and a chapel. I went into the chapel, and explored, and sang a few songs. I left the chapel and saw a red arrow sign nailed to a tree. I gleefully began to follow the signs and explore. It wasn't long before I found myself in a dark, swamp-like place and I could hear mosquitoes buzzing all around me. I was terrified because I am so allergic to mosquito bites. I felt the sting of the first bite and started to pray, asking God to protect me from being bitten any more. Although the pests were all around me, I didn't receive another bite.

From this dark place I stepped out into a clearing with the most beautiful wild flowers I have ever seen. They were everywhere, bathing the world in color and good cheer. I sat down among them and soaked in the diversity and grandeur of God's creation. It felt as though God had created this place just for me, and I didn't want to leave. It wasn't until I thought I heard chickens clucking that I was able to tear myself away from this beautiful place. I rounded a bend and saw a chicken pen, but it was empty. I headed back to my cabin.

My evening meal was just as simple as the place where I sat to enjoy it in my cabin: cheese, bread and fruit. It was wonderfully delicious. My meal was disturbed when the mosquito bite on my arm began relentlessly itching. I had no bite medicine and was beginning to feel miserable. I went into the sitting area, set up my CD player and popped one of the CD's in that I had brought along. I lay on the couch listening to the music and itching. I raised my arm into the air and left it hanging there as I thanked God that I only had one bite. I asked him to heal that one and take away the itch and pain. I don't know how long I laid there, but my arm hung in the air effortlessly until the CD ended. As I lowered it, there was no sign of a bite, nothing.

I slept well that night with a full stomach and full heart from the blessings of that day. The next morning, following my simple breakfast, I headed to the chapel to pray. There was a beautiful stained-glass cross with the sign of the United Methodist Church hanging there. This was a Catholic camp so I was surprised to see that symbol there that was so precious to me. I lit a candle of thanksgiving and left the chapel by the same door I came in. This exit provided me with a different point of view and I could see a large pond nearby.

I slowly walked around the pond and ended up sitting under a great big tree at one end. I thought how it's roots that were above the ground on either side of me felt like arms encircling me. I prayed for a bit and then began to meditate on a familiar scripture, "Be still and know that I am God".[10] My meditation broke down the phrase into seven parts:

Be

Be still

Be still and

Be still and know

Be still and know that

Be still and know that I AM

Be still and know that I AM GOD.

My eyes were closed. I held my hands in my lap, palms up and recited this scripture in this pattern over and over again. Soon I heard a response for each line from the Holy Spirit:

Be (just be, don't do)

Be still (don't rush, don't worry)

Be still and (there is more to life)

Be still and know (I am going to reveal something to you)

Be still and know that (that something is all you need know)

---

[10] Psalm 46:10

> Be still and know that I AM (I am the great I AM, the alpha and the omega, the beginning and end)
>
> Be still and know that I AM GOD (there is no other God besides me)

I opened my eyes and waited. Then I felt the Holy Spirit say, "Come and walk with me." I stood up and began walking and God's presence was palpable. I was not alone. I walked by a stream that fed the pond and there were hundreds of little tiny frogs hopping about. It was delightful. A cool breeze brushed through my hair. I felt filled from the tips of my toes to the top of my head with love.

Continuing to walk alongside the stream I found another pond, this one secluded with a wooden bench for onlookers to enjoy. I climbed upon the bench and it was so high my feet didn't touch the ground. I felt like a little girl as I swung my legs back and forth to the rhythm of frogs croaking nearby. Little fish swirled around in the pond and dragonflies darted about looking for larvae for lunch. Birds came to bathe and serenaded at the joy of a simple bath. It was glorious! I felt the Holy Spirit come over me and fill me with a great joy.

Returning to my cabin I was hungry and tired, so I grabbed a PB&J sandwich and some fruit and sat down with a good book on the porch. Soon I fell asleep. When I awoke I wondered if everything that I had experienced that morning was a dream. I checked my arm for the place where there had been a mosquito bite 24 hours before. I felt as if I had been given the greatest of gifts that day: sign of the church, time with God, a walk with Jesus, praising God with his creation.

On my final day, Sunday morning, I headed out for my usual walk and noticed that there were fields of grain behind my cabin. They were ripe for harvest. I climbed upon a turnstile and watched the grain wave back and forth in the wind. I asked out loud, "Jesus do you love me?" I heard this answer, "I love you as much as the twelve that I walked on this earth with." I cried and cried. When I finished crying I knew it was time to head home.

As I recount these three days here, the feelings of the love of God rise in me again as if it just happened today. I will never forget the closeness I felt to God, Jesus and the Holy Spirit that weekend, and the miraculous ways in which he revealed his love to me.

Miracle of Friends

1 Corinthians 1:3-4 (NLT)

"All praise to the God and Father of our Lord Jesus Christ. He is the source of every mercy and the God who comforts us. He comforts us in all our troubles so that we can comfort others. When others are troubled, we are able to give them the same comfort God has given us."

This is the story of four very different women. I have been privileged to have many women friends throughout my life, and through my friendship with these four, it is evident to me that they were the direct result of God's actions in my life.

*****

I met Renae over my brother's fence one day when I was mowing his lawn at the farm in Cleburne, Texas. Renae was his across-the-road neighbor, who had a dachshund puppy she was trying to sell. The next time I saw her was when one of her hogs escaped and tore up our garden. It wasn't until the tragic day that her husband died that I really began to know her. My brother, Max had called me and told me that his neighbor had died suddenly, and I felt the Holy Spirit nudge me to reach out to Renae. I scrambled around my kitchen looking for something to cook and ended up loading an ice chest with bits and pieces such as spaghetti and pork chops.

I delivered the food and the next day Renae called to thank me for caring. She invited me to go to the florist with her to pick out her husband's casket spray. I felt this was highly unusual since we had barely met but agreed to go with her. Max and I attended her husband's funeral and I thought "that's that." However, Renae wouldn't let me go. We had snow cones in the park while she showed me a photo album that she had managed to rescue from a housefire. She opened up to me as she opened the book and I learned of the difficult life that she and her four sons shared.

One day in my home, we were talking about shoes. She said that her sister always told her that she had "clodhopper" feet because she wore a size ten shoe. When I revealed that I wore a size ten as well, we bonded. As we laughed she referred to herself as a "rolling walnut". I said, "Well, if you're a walnut, I'm a peanut." That stuck! From then on, we were Peanut and Wally.

We have been friends since 1999. I love her. I love her sons as if they were my own children. We have taught each other many life lessons and shared the ups and downs of life over this time. My friendship with Renae is a miracle because God used her to teach me to be a better, less judgmental, open- hearted person. Our miraculous relationship can best be described by something Renae once told me: "When you share a sorrow, you half it. When you share a joy, you double it."

*****

Alice and I first met at an assembly of the Central Texas Conference of the United Methodist Church in Fort Worth, Texas. I had known of her husband, Jimmy, since we had joined a church in Cleburne, Texas where her husband was the former pastor. I felt an instant draw to her, and when she hugged me, it felt like she sealed some sort of deal.

In 2006 while my daughter-in-law and I were searching for a new church home, I found Alice sitting in a pew at the First Christian Church in Cleburne, and felt as if I had found a long-ago, lost friend. We joined that church and Alice and I grew to love each other deeply, while learning that many events in our lives were very similar. One time, we traveled to hear Christian motivational speaker Lisa Welchel, who had been a star in the 1980's TV series *The Facts of Life*, give her testimony. She told about her closest friend "Emmit", whom she could always turn to for advice and wise counsel. Alice and I began calling each other by that name with little girl giggles. Another nickname Alice claimed for us is "Anam Cara" which is Irish for "soul friend". Yes, even our souls are tied together.

We have taught Sunday School together and were called to be church elders at the same time. She has driven me (her spiritual gift) to Arkansas to visit Steve when he was ill, and she and Jimmy drove with Ed, Rufus (our dog) and I across country when we moved from Texas to Idaho. She came to visit me when I found out I had cancer, and I sat by her side when Jimmy was gravely ill from kidney cancer. She has hugged me into wholeness many times. Alice is a miraculous love gift of God to me, and I believe she would say I was a gift to her.

*****

In Troy, Idaho I opened a children's used clothing store. I had a regular customer, named Marilyn who owned the antique store in town. She came in from time-to-time looking for items that she might be able to resell in her own store. I barely knew her name, but I did discover at our first meeting that we had something in common: her sister lived in Cleburne, Texas.

In 2014 I had participated in a Bible Study called "First Steps" which was designed to introduce non-believers (or shaky believers) to Jesus. I was so excited about this study that I wanted to share it with the world. I made a list of 30 people, whom I knew to be unchurched and/or non-believers in Troy, to invite to a "First Steps" study group. I must admit that I did all of this without consulting God even once. I bought 15 books and began working my list. One day Marilyn walked into my store and I heard God say, "Invite her." I was very nervous, but I did ask. I was surprised that she seemed interested, as I handed her a book.

On the evening when the group was scheduled to meet, I squeezed 15 chairs into my small living room and waited. The time came to begin, and no one was there. A few minutes later, a car pulled up in front of the house and after a few minutes more, I saw Marilyn emerge and come toward the house. I was both excited and embarrassed. Since she was the only person to show up, I felt like she might think it was all a set-up and leave. I greeted her and offered her an easy-out, pointing out the obvious, that no one else was there. She said she wanted to stay.

Over the next several weeks, Marilyn, Ed and I went through the "First Steps" book. She revealed how "something" was happening in her life that compelled her to want more. From this study Marilyn joined us and some of our Troy neighbors for one Bible study after another. I spent time with her in her antique shop, visiting about our studies and life. I greatly admired her adventurous spirit and loved hearing about her yoga classes, music lessons, and hikes around the world.

I have grown to love Marilyn as a sister-in-Christ. The fact that the Holy Spirit arranged our friendship through "First Steps" is truly a miracle.

*****

In 2015 we changed churches, and I was delighted that some Troy friends, Aaron and Francie Tyler, were already members there. Aaron was on fire to serve the Lord. One Sunday he brought in a speaker from Celebrate Recovery, and that young woman expressed a need for volunteers to help cook meals for their meetings. This sparked an interest in me and I convinced Ed that we should volunteer.

The meetings were held at a church not far away on Friday evenings with about 60 people in attendance. Ed and I arrived early and helped another couple prepare spaghetti for the crowd. After the meal they began singing praises to God and their voices were not like those of an ordinary church gathering. They sounded like people who meant what they were singing. I listened to their explanation of what Celebrate Recovery was all about from the kitchen as we worked to clean up. I felt drawn to come again, and to participate.

The next Friday evening as Ed and I drove toward the church we passed a trailer park where my estranged daughter, Amanda and her children were living. I wondered if Celebrate Recovery would have the answers I needed about why and how Amanda's life was so distorted. We sat alone at a table with our meal. I looked up at the entrance and saw a woman, about my age, walk through the door and our eyes locked. She came straight to me, and for a moment I wondered if she was an angel. She said, "Is this seat taken?" I told her it wasn't, and she placed her items down on the table and went to get her food.

When Rachel returned she told me her story about why she had come to Celebrate Recovery four years earlier. She had a broken daughter, who was Amanda's age, and needed some answers. Her story was so similar to mine that I couldn't believe what I was hearing. Scripture tells us "God works for the good of those who love him, who have been called according to his purpose."[11] God indeed was at work in my attending Celebrate Recovery and through my new friendship with Rachel.

A common bond of brokenness, pain and suffering hardly seems like a miracle, but the love I have for Rachel would not exist without those things in our lives and I am truly grateful.

---

[11] Romans 8:28

Miracles of Life After Death

Deuteronomy 29:29a (NIV)

"The secret things belong to the LORD our God, but the things revealed belong to us and to our children forever..."

      I always wanted a brother, from the time I was a little girl. When I was only two or three years old I had an imaginary friend, "Mike", and I believed he was my brother. In reality, I was an only child until I was almost eleven years old. When my brother Max was born, I felt closer to him than a sister, and thought he hung the moon. In 1992, when I found my two brothers, George and Steve, I felt like I must be among the most blessed people on earth.

      With deep love, comes deep heartache at its parting.

*****

      Early on the morning of February 1, 1997, my phone rang, and it was my brother Steve calling to tell me that our brother George had died in the night of a massive heart attack. I dropped the phone, and flailed about on my bed, screaming in agony, and hoping that it wasn't true. I took my daughter Samantha with me and we hurried to George's home in Roland, Oklahoma. Funeral arrangements were made, grave site was selected, chores were run, condolences were paid by friends and neighbors, nothing consoling me. Two days after his death, I walked out the front door of his home, across the little footbridge, and headed toward my car, my head hanging in grief. I lifted my head to see George standing there, against a tree, in his jeans and red flannel shirt, hand lifting a pipe to his lips, for a last draw of cherry tobacco. I gasped in disbelief, covered my face with my hands, and stood immobilized. Seconds later when I gained my courage, I uncovered my face and he was gone.

      Months of grieving went by and my loss was compounded by the fear that George was not a believer in Jesus. Then one night I had a dream. I dreamt that a black wall phone was ringing. I answered it and it was George, already dead. He asked to speak to Steve. I called Steve to come to the phone and as he heard George's voice he smiled with delight. Then he passed the phone to our father and his own mother, Mary, before it was returned to him and he hung up. I was very disappointed because I didn't get to talk to my brother. Then the phone rang a second time. Again, it was George. He said, "Karen, I want you to know that I love you and so does God." I believe this was more than a dream-wish, but God comforting his child to let me know that George was with him.

In 2013 a great tragedy occurred. The mother of George's son, Christopher, was in an explosion in her home. There was no doubt in Christopher's mind that his mother had a strong faith, when in the midst of her suffering and pain she could say, "God is good." She died in June and Christopher's grief was very great. He longed to hear her voice and needed reassurance.

One day Christopher and I were chatting on the computer, when he voiced to me concerns about his father's salvation. I decided it was time to share with him the dream I had where George called me. There was no response from Chris for several minutes and I wondered if I had offended him. Then he started to type again. He told me that what I told him made the hair stand up on the back of his neck. He said he had recently had a dream where a red telephone was ringing. When he picked it up, it was his mother, calling from heaven to tell him that she loved him and was safe with God.

*****

Max called and said that he had some news and was coming to see me. As I recall it was 2007, when I watched him and his wife, Mairead, walk up the sidewalk to my front door, clutching each other as if the earth was going to open up and swallow them. We stood face-to-face at the doorway and I knew that they had grim news. Cancer. Max had been coughing for several months and he had finally gone to the doctor. He had stage four lung cancer.

One day in May 2009 I went to Sonic Drive-In (Burleson, Texas) to read and pray for Max's healing, while my granddaughter

Kamryn was at tutoring. I was reading from John 11, the story of Lazarus, Mary and Martha's brother, being raised from the dead. As I read, God told me, "Max will die." My phone rang. It was Mairead. She said that Max had been taken to the hospital, and she thought he had a heart attack. I picked up Kamryn and we drove back to Cleburne. When I got to the hospital, Mairead told me that she and Max were having a milkshake at Sonic in Cleburne, when suddenly he couldn't breathe.

Max had pneumonia and was intubated to sustain his life. The doctor told us that even if they could heal the pneumonia, he would still have lung cancer, and suggested that Mairead make the decision to take him off life support. He was in the hospital a week before she agreed to this. One day I stepped into his room and rubbed healing oil on his body, as I cried out to God in my prayer language, asking him to help Max take the next step. Max was not in that body. I believe he was watching me from right above his body as I prayed and rubbed him with the aromatic oil.

It took almost two years for cancer to finally take Max's life. How grateful I am that, unlike George, I had a lot of time to tell him that I loved him dearly. He died on June 4, 2009.

*****

Steve told me that he had AIDS, and that he had begun searching for me after learning that he was ill, not knowing how much time he would have left. At first, he seemed healthy but over the years he had a heart attack, Non-Hodgkin's Lymphoma, and face cancer which began to spread into other parts of his body.

I went to Van Buren, Arkansas in December 2015 to say goodbye. We had a wonderful weekend together reminiscing, crying, hoping. He and I had been so close, even though our relationship had had its ups and downs over the last 23 years. I couldn't believe I was about to lose my third brother.

Steve died March 6, 2016. Grasping for one last bit of Steve, I opened his Facebook page that day. His last post was dated March 6, a share about "Arya's Eyes" (*Game of Thrones*). The very day he died it was posted, and he was not physically able to do that! I knew this was a message to me. You see, since 1992 when we first met, we would look into each other's eyes and he would say, "We have twin eyes." But was I deceiving myself? I still longed to hear from him one last time. That very week, I walked into my bedroom and as I crossed in front of a loaded-down knick-knack shelf, something flew off in front of me, hitting the floor at my feet. It was a music box that Steve had given me. Nothing else came off the shelf, only that tiny wooden box which played one of Steve's favorite songs, *Wind Beneath My Wings*.

*****

Jesus made strong promises to us about life after death and they are a great comfort when you lose a loved one, if you also believe. "Let not your heart be troubled; ye believe in God, believe also in me... I go to prepare a place for you. And If I go and prepare a place for you, I will come again, and receive you unto myself; that where I am, there ye may be also."[12] Because of my belief in Jesus, and God the Father, the promise keeper, I desire one final miracle: when I make my way through Heaven's Gates, I hope to see Jesus first, then my three brothers there, waiting to welcome me home.

---

[12] 12 John 14:3 (KJV)

Miracle of Connection

Hebrews 12:1 (NIV)

"Therefore, since we are surrounded by such a great cloud of witnesses, let us throw off everything that hinders and the sin that so easily entangles. And let us run with perseverance the race marked out for us."

In 2016 I asked God to give me a Word for the year. That year he gave me the word "content", with this scripture, "I know what it is to be in need, and I know what it is to have plenty. I have learned the secret of being content in any and every situation, whether well fed or hungry, whether living in plenty or in want. I can do all this through him who gives me strength."[13] In March of that year I contracted a virus which caused my already diseased kidneys to begin to shut down. By September I was on dialysis. I often reminded myself during that time, that I was very blessed to be 64 years old, with my kidneys functioning fine until now. I trusted God with this change in my life and relied on Jesus to give me the strength that I needed. I even felt content in March of that year when my brother Steve died. I felt a peace beyond my understanding.[14]

2017 rolled around and once again I asked God for a Word. This time I heard "connect". We started off the year with some challenges. On a Friday in January I received the news that I had breast cancer. Two days later we had a chimney fire. I needed inspiration to keep focused on Jesus, so I began to make a "Hope Book" for myself. In this book are many pages listing the ways that God connected me with others in 2017, as they came forward to support my family and love on me. They cooked meals, made gifts, sent cards, made prayer blankets, traveled a long way to visit, sent books, offered to donate a kidney, brought me flowers, invited me to attend support groups, shoveled snow, babysat Surinity, and on

---

[13] Philippians 4:12-13
[14] Philippians 4:7

and on. Although these were very important to sustaining me, they weren't miraculous. But this was...

In May 2016 we attended Evangelical Free Church in Pullman, Washington for the first time. I chose a random seat, and immediately the woman next to me introduced herself, Treva Worthington. We began sharing information and I soon learned that Treva lived in Troy. She invited me to a Bible Study that she and her husband led in Troy, but I never attended because of lack of energy or enthusiasm.

I was struggling with so many things besides my health challenges for months. My house was disheveled, dirty, and unorganized. I thought about it every day, and I wished I had the energy to get up and do something to change this. I didn't specifically pray about it, but I dwelled on it and felt so anxious. One day Treva called me and said that she wanted to come clean my house. My pride wanted me to respond, "No way!" But my need overcame my pride and I agreed. Treva told me that God told her to come clean my house. She faithfully cleaned my house for several weeks, and then her daughter Heather came to help out as well. As she cleaned, and we talked, we became good friends.

About the same time that God prompted Treva to reach out to me, I got a card from my friend Lena Gipson. Lena and I were school mates and graduated together from Crowley High School (Crowley, Texas). Lena wrote that she wished she lived close enough to bring me a meal, but since that wasn't possible, she was sending me a check so that I could get someone to help clean my house, or anything else I might need. Miraculous? I believe so. Amazing? Definitely.

Miracle of Invictus

John 1:16 (NIV)

"From the fullness of His grace we have all received one blessing after another."

The Troy Bible Study at Bill and Treva Worthington's home has blessed me in so many ways. Not only have I made good friends with the three couples that I study with, but I have had new insight week after week into God's love for us. In the winter of 2017 this was the case as we studied Charles Swindoll's book *The Grace Awakening*. Chapter 2 included a poem, that none of us had ever heard, although Dr. Swindoll said it was very famous. I read the poem and the author's comments without anything noteworthy coming to mind.

A couple of days later, my son Eddy had a dream that he couldn't wait to share:

February 23, 2917 2:00 a.m.

"I just woke up from a dream. I and someone else were in a snowstorm. We could see off in the distance that some sort of a snow tornado was heading our way. Once it was upon us, I kept saying 'Invictus' and as it neared and swooped me up, I was embraced by it and lifted up into the sky (flying) ... I woke up then. So I looked up Invictus... All I can say is awesome!"

Eddy called me and told me about his dream, and I told him that the poem *Invictus* was in our Bible Study book just a couple of days ago. "What could this all mean?" we jointly wondered.

I told my daughter Samantha about Eddy's dream and the poem *Invictus*. The next day she was driving to school in Lewiston, Idaho when she heard "Invictus" on the radio. She didn't catch the whole radio spot because her ears could not let loose of that by now very familiar name, "Invictus".

54

Ed and I planned a visit with Eddy and his family in Florida in the fall. The week before we were scheduled to leave great hurricanes were battering the Caribbean Islands and heading toward the southeastern United States. Hurricane Irma was making a bee-line toward Florida and was classified as a level 5. We joined all of Florida and many others in praying and asking God to spare Florida, while Eddy prepared his family and home for the storm.

Eddy had recently been injured at work, tearing his bicep. Although he had this terrible injury, he managed to make a bunker room in his house and used ladders to sturdy exterior walls. He released his boat from its trailer and tied it to a tree so that it would be easily accessible in case of flooding. He checked his emergency food supply. He locked himself down along with his three children and his girlfriend Shawna, and they prepared to wait out the storm. Through it all, he remembered *Invictus*, that he was "master of his own fate."

By the time Irma reached shore its power reduced and as it reached my son's house it was recategorized to a 2. The family lost the screens off their pool cover and a few trees but suffered no further damage. They were without power for over a week, yet they were able to take care of themselves and their neighbors, providing food and other assistance.

Eddy's prophetic dream, along with Samantha's and my affirmations, is now part of our family story. It was miraculous that God heard our prayers and caused the hurricane to lose its power, but it was even more miraculous that Eddy was prepared to be the captain of his fate, in response to God's revelation.

INVICTUS

Out of the night that covers me,
Black as the Pit from pole to pole,
I thank whatever gods may be
For my unconquerable soul.

In the fell clutch of circumstance
I have not winced nor cried aloud.
Under the bludgeonings of chance
My head is bloody, but unbowed.
Beyond this place of wrath and tears
Looms but the Horror of the shade,
And yet the menace of the years
Finds, and shall find, me unafraid.

It matters not how strait the gate,
How charged with punishments the scroll.
I am the master of my fate:
I am the captain of my soul.

-- William Ernest Henley (1888)

Miracles of Idaho

Luke 18:29-30 (NIV)

"'Truly I tell you,' Jesus replied, 'no one who has left home or brothers or sisters or mother or father or children or fields for me and the gospel will fail to receive a hundred times as much in this present age … and in the age to come eternal life.'"

Ed: "I want to move north."

Me: "No."

Ed: " I believe God is telling me that we should move

north."

Me: "God has never spoken to you! He only speaks to me."

That is how this journey all began. Ed and I had been married almost 40 years and had lived together in nine states. His wanting to move was nothing new. Usually I was agreeable, but this time I was putting my foot down. We had lived in Cleburne, Texas for 11 years and I was finally feeling at home. When he brought God into the mix, I honestly thought he had to be mistaken. I prayed about it and as I was praying I heard God say, "Listen to your husband." I went to Ed immediately and apologized to him for not listening, and not believing, and agreed to move if he said so. Ed told me that while he wasn't certain at all about the direction to take, he kept hearing God say, "Just take a step."

Ed's first inclination was that we should move to Colorado, in particularly Pagosa Springs. We made a trip there and it was lovely, but Ed knew right away that this wasn't God's plan. As 2011 rolled around, Ed continued investigating and researching locations for our new home, while I was pursuing other things. I was helping lead a Healing Ministry at Cleburne's First Christian Church and was seeking some direction. I learned about the International Healing Rooms Ministry in Spokane, Washington and a training that they were conducting in July. I went to Ed with this news and he replied, "Good. I can take a look around Idaho while you are attending that conference." Idaho? Idaho had never crossed my mind and I was curious about why he would pick that location.

Somewhere between our decision to move and July, Ed and I started daydreaming about starting a thrift store business wherever we moved. Ed was wanting to sell "survival-type" items and camping gear. We bought a guidebook for starting a thrift store, and it suggested locating near a college town where you could sell, buy and resell to college students. For this reason, he focused his attention on Moscow, Idaho, home of the University of Idaho, and neighboring city Pullman, Washington, where Washington State University was located.

July finally came, and we headed to Spokane. Ed and I attended the healing conference in Spokane together. During the conference, we went to the prayer rooms for prayer. A trio of volunteers greeted us as we walked into the little room that was thick with the Presence of the Holy Spirit. One of my requests was for pain relief in my aching hip. As Ed and I stood side-by-side with the prayer warrior in front, she prayed, and I felt my leg lengthen out. It was as if it had been drawn up in the socket forever and now released. The pain was still there, but now I had a noticeably longer leg.[15] The final person to pray for us, an older man, had us hold hands. He said, "Step forward. God is telling me that you need to just keep taking a step." Ed and I looked at each other in disbelief. This man also said that we had had a difficult road with our children, but that our marriage would become a strong example to many.

At the end of the training, we then headed out to explore the Palouse region of the northwest. The countryside looked like a painting come to life. We arrived at harvest time and the landscape was spotted with tractors pulling equipment to harvest acres and acres of wheat. Pine trees outlined the rolling hills and I was drawn into the beauty all around us. We had arranged to meet a realtor, Teri Skiles to show us a house. When we met we quickly discovered

---

[15] When I returned to Texas and went to the orthopedic doctor he commented on how much longer my right leg was than my left. It is a full 3 cm longer.

that she and her husband had a thrift store in nearby Potlatch, Idaho and made an instant connection as a result. The house we had hoped for was under contract, so Teri began showing us other properties near Moscow, Idaho. We found a home that I fell In love with in the little community of Troy, and Teri also showed us a potential location for our thrift store. We made an offer on the house and returned to Texas.

Now we had not informed anyone, neither friends or family, of our impending move. When we returned to Texas we told our best friends Alice and Jimmy Finley first, then our pastor and his wife. All four affirmed our calling to move for ministry in the north. At dinner with Alice and Jimmy, I mentioned that we might have difficulty being approved for a mortgage on the Idaho house since we had not sold our house in Cleburne. Jimmy told us that he had just heard from an old friend, a mortgage broker in Oregon, and thought perhaps he could help us out. A phone call to Jimmy's friend secured our new home.

One night I dreamed about preparing to move to Idaho. We were looking for items for our thrift store by going to people's homes who had just had garage sales and asking them if they had leftovers that we might have for our store. One lady met me at her door and said that she did have something for us. From her doorway she went to my left and came back with two large black garbage bags full of buttons. When I awoke I looked online to see what buttons meant in a dream. The site I checked said buttons represented clothes, or course, and riches beyond what money could buy.

When the time came for us to move, Ed gave his employer a two-week notice on a Friday. Because of the sensitive nature of his work, his expectation was that they would thank him for giving notice and let him go immediately. Surprisingly his supervisor thanked him and said nothing. On Monday morning he was called into the supervisor's office and he couldn't believe what he was hearing. They asked him to continue to work for them, from Idaho, for half the time and the same pay he was making. This was a big "sign" from God that we were moving in the right direction.

I had hip replacement surgery in August but managed to push through to get packed for our big move. A week before we departed I went to say goodbye to my good friend, Cheri Utley. I told her that we were following God's call to move to Idaho and we were opening a thrift store. Before I left, she asked me to wait because she had something for me. I watched my dream about buttons play out before my eyes. She left her doorway, walked to the left, and came back with two large black trash bags full of baby clothes that her little girl had outgrown. She said, "Maybe you can use these in your store." I realized immediately that Cheri was the woman from my dream. I took the clothes home and began going through the bags. It dawned on me that perhaps our thrift store could serve the community more with good children's clothing rather than survival stuff.

At the end of October, we were on the road to Idaho. Alice and Jimmy Finley drove with us and helped us make the 1,900-mile journey. We quickly settled in and by March of 2012 were ready to open our store. The plan was that I would buy clothing from customers and resell the clothing, ministering to the needs of people coming and going.

I had truly believed that we would arrive in Idaho and God would give us a big assignment. I could only imagine that if he would have us pick up and move away from our home, friends and family that there must be a really BIG reason, and I kept looking for it. The store gave me an opportunity to meet many people in the community and for them to begin to trust us, although we were newcomers, *but* big ministry it definitely wasn't. Although I managed the business to the best of my ability, the hours of sitting alone certainly didn't feel like ministry.

Ed's long-distance job with his Texas employer lasted about a year. We prayed that God would give him a job with a testimony. He began to job search again, interviewing with both universities. No offer was made, but in April 2013, the man who interviewed him for the University of Idaho position called. He said he had a friend that was looking for a part-time computer tech and felt that Ed would be a good fit. He interviewed, was hired and in the first week went from part-time tech to future full-time computer center manager for Eco Analysts. This was a company owned by Christians where Ed could flourish and they were to be a great support in the years to come.

In Troy, as I began to make friends, two people that I really connected with were Holly Stoolfire (Sombret) and Mark McCune. The three of us felt a calling to reach out in the Name of Jesus to the people of Troy. I thought that perhaps this was the big thing that I was sent to Idaho for. In June of 2014 we sponsored three events under the name Pete's Place.[16] There were about 50 people at the first two events, which featured gaming, live music, free food, and a speaker for the Lord. The third event was held at the Troy City Park and was focused on choosing life rather than abortion. We partnered with Palouse Care Network and showed the movie *October Baby*. About 160 people came to eat the free food, listen to live music and hear what we had to say.

Through it all I knew that was not the big thing I was waiting for. I now know that I could not force the hand of God to show me what his purpose was in bringing us to Idaho. I recalled learning about "more" in the Kingdom of God meaning either something "bigger" or a multitude of "little" things. I began to recognize that the little things were just as impactful as big ones when I tried to start a study group in my home. I invited 30 people, and only one person showed up, the one that the Holy Spirit drew to me.

I closed the store in June of 2014. We joined a different church after I had a falling out with the pastor of the church we belonged to in Troy. We brought my daughter Amanda and her two children to live with us from Texas and then watched them leave in anger. Things were changing for me. In 2015 we began attending Celebrate Recovery and in time I became a member of the leadership team. I volunteered at Palouse Care Network and became a mentor at Hope Center. At the end of 2014 my daughter

---

[16] A long-time Troy resident had desired to establish a place for youth to be ministered to under this name, but it had never come to fruition.

Samantha and her two children moved from Oklahoma to live with us.

For a long time, Samantha had wanted to go into a medical field. Once she was in Idaho and able to see a future, she decided to train in Radiology Technology at Lewis Clark State College in Lewiston, Idaho. One of her required classes was Communications. Samantha was very uneasy when she began this class and learned that she had to make several speeches throughout the semester. One of those speeches was a persuasive speech and she decided early on that she would speak to the issue of choosing life over abortion. With every speech she prepared she struggled with finding the courage to speak it aloud to me let alone in front of a class of 30 or so.

She was so anxious about the abortion speech above all others, yet she put more time into it than all the others combined. She made posters, she did research, she went to see a speaker who had worked for Planned Parenthood, she made a power-point presentation, she rehearsed in front of me, and in front of my friends. She even practiced how she would address questions, should anyone have any. Finally the day came for her to present to the class. Her teacher was so impressed with her presentation and choice of topic that she asked Samantha if she would consider entering a schoolwide speech contest. Samantha said, "No."

Samantha's teacher was a Christian and she knew that Samantha's message needed to be delivered, so she urged her to enter the contest. Samantha began to accept the idea and decided to enter. She asked me to help her by running her computer. We bought her a new outfit to wear and she rehearsed day-after-day. The night of the contest there were 80-90 students in attendance, most of them there because they could get class credit for attending. There were about 8 speakers and a panel of 5 judges. We listened to speeches on the benefits of exercise, the dangers of texting while driving, and other non-impacting topics. Samantha's speech was last.

The Holy Spirit started moving as Samantha took the stage. She presented with ease and grace the facts about abortion, and why the listeners should choose life. From my advantage point I could see the audience lean in, with their eyes locked on her. Some cried. Some looked stunned. Some crumbled. As she concluded her presentation, it was question time. As she had expected one of the first questions that was asked was, "Why are you so passionate about this?" She took a deep breath, moved across the stage and said, "When I was 19 I was raped. I chose to keep my baby, and I have a beautiful daughter." More questions were asked of her than any other speaker.

Then it was time to vote. Both students and judges had input. While waiting for the voting results, several people, including instructors, came up to congratulate her and thank her for her presentation and vulnerability. One young man asked if he could hug her. In the hallway a girl said that she had just learned that she was pregnant and now she would choose life. The voting results were read. Samantha won the judges' votes and the students'! I was one proud momma, but I also saw God's hand in it all. Maybe this was why we were in Idaho. Maybe it wasn't about us at all.

I continued to volunteer. I trained to be a *Genesis Process*[17] counselor and worked the process with three women over the next year. Then in 2016 my kidneys began to fail, my energy evaporated, and my path took a big twist. By September 2016 I was on dialysis, and in January 2017 I learned that I had breast cancer. I dropped out of my volunteer rolls and waited on God. My momma always said, "This too shall pass," and I held onto that. I felt like people were watching me even as I dealt with the health problems, and that God could certainly use me in a new way. At one time God had told me, "I can use your life to lead others to me, and I can even use your death to draw others to me." I was convinced that he was going to use my illnesses to draw others to him as well.

---

[17] "Genesis Process provides a Biblical and neurochemical understanding of what is broken and causes self-destruction." Genesisprocess.org

In 2017 my family began to discuss what our plans would be after Samantha graduated. We all agreed that it was time to move to Texas and be near my son Zach and closer to my son Eddy. One thought that kept me wondering if this was the right thing to do was how much I trusted and loved my healthcare team, Dr. Todd my primary doctor, Dr. Kristie Jones my kidney doctor, and Melanie Holdren my dialysis nurse. I prayed and asked God to help me believe moving back to Texas was the right thing to do. Those who know me will find this amusing because I have been saying I want to move back to Texas almost since the day I set foot in Idaho. I missed my home, my sons, my friends, my church, the landscape, the food, the theater, everything. Maybe my clinging to my heath care team was my way of finding solace if God decided we shouldn't move back. Then Dr. Todd left her practice to start a practice of her own. Next Melanie left to work in orthopedics. I felt released.

The last thing that was keeping me in Idaho was my grandchildren, Amanda's children. Then in the spring of 2018, God put that in order and I was reconciled to them and able to see hope for their future, and felt I could move, knowing that they would be taken care of.

I cannot count the many "little"s that we've been blessed by while living in Idaho: work, friends, huckleberry picking, worshipping, growing… Moving here was not just some whim, but truly God miraculously speaking into Ed's life, and therefore mine and many others.

Conclusion

Since I was a child I have wondered about the world, my place in it and why I was so fortunate. I would lie in bed and think, "Why wasn't I born poor, or a member of a persecuted race? Why do I have a mother who loves me, a nice home and plenty to eat?" And now as an adult, like King David of the Old Testament of the Bible, I still wonder, "Who am I Sovereign LORD, and what is my family that you have brought me this far?"[18]

I am an ordinary woman, who would have a very ordinary story except for this one thing: God. I have always believed in not only God's existence, but also his presence. I truly believe that God desires to be in a relationship with each of us, not simply worshipped from afar. I was privileged to start my relationship very early in life, but no matter how old you are, it's never too late to ask Jesus to walk with you through life and demonstrate his powers and mighty miracles.

A word about grace...

I am not particularly religious. I have been rebellious, and I have had seasons of doubt and questioning. Grace is when God fills in the gaps of our failures and keeps us connected to him. Grace is unlimited and probably the cornerstone of being able to detect God's power and miracles in our lives. We have to believe that God loves us, wants the best for us, and is always looking out for us. He will move mountains to help us fulfill His purpose for us and in us.

To my family...

Psalm 89:1-2

"I will sing of the LORD's great love forever; with my mouth I will make your faithfulness known through all generations. I will declare that your love stands firm forever, that you have established your faithfulness in heaven itself."

---

[18] 2 Samuel 7:18

These stories have been preserved for each of you to remind you that we serve a powerful, miracle-making God. Tell them to your children and grandchildren, and don't forget to keep sharing how God is working in your own life to the generations to come.

"And now I entrust you to God and the Word of His grace...with His message that is able to build you up and give you an inheritance with all those he has set apart for himself." Acts 20:32

Edwin "Eddy", Shawna, Karalee, Owen, Chloe

Zachary "Zach", Mary Ann, Ariel,
Kristan, Clayton and Nyla Belle,
Hadley, Westin

Amanda, Kamryn, Matthew

Samantha, Shayla, Surinity "Suri"